CW01572747

1. a) Homeostasis is the maintenance o
   b) It is achieved by balancing bodily
      waste products.

2. a)–b) In any order.
   a) Temperature b) Water

3. The consequence could be death.

4. a) i) 1200cm³ ii) 150cm³ iii) 1350cm³ iv) 300cm³
   b) i) The body will produce sweat. ii) The body will produce less urine.

5. a) As they exercise their body temperature goes up. The body
      produces sweat in order to cool the body down.
   b) They need to drink plenty of water to replace the water that has
      been lost as sweat.

6. Hypothermia.

Page 5

1. a) i)–ii) In any order. Accept any other suitable answers.
      i) Premature babies. ii) People with kidney failure.
   b) Accept any suitable answer.

2. a)–c) In any order.
   a) Lack of oxygen b) Low temperatures c) Getting rid of waste
   gases (e.g. carbon dioxide).

3. Scuba equipment controls the gases entering the body and ensures
   that oxygen is kept at the correct level.

4. The low pressure makes it difficult to breathe.

5. To replace water and essential salts that have been lost through sweat.

6. Negative feedback is when two receptors control the level of
   something, e.g. temperature. In an incubator, if the temperature level
   goes too high, a receptor turns the heat off, and if the temperature
   level falls too low a receptor turns the heat back on.

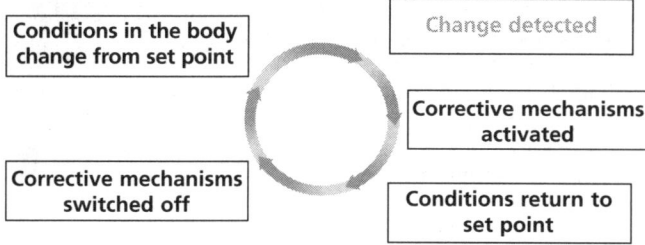

Conditions in the body change from set point

Change detected

Corrective mechanisms activated

Corrective mechanisms switched off

Conditions return to set point

Page 6

1. Diffusion is the movement of particles though a semi-permeable
   membrane from a high concentration to a low concentration.

2. Plants will absorb nitrates from the soil into their root hairs by
   diffusion.

3. Osmosis is the diffusion of water from a high to a low concentration.

4. The pure water solution is more dilute than the sugar solution, so
   water moves by osmosis across the partially permeable visking tubing
   into the thistle funnel making the water level in the funnel rise.

5. b, e, f

6. The water inside the plants' cells will be in a higher concentration
   than in the sea water outside the cells. Water will therefore move out
   of the cells by osmosis. Because the cells do not then contain enough
   water, they will wilt.

Pages 7–8

1. a i)–ii) In any order.
      i) If the cell loses too much water, it will not be able to carry out
         its chemical reactions.
      ii) If too much water enters the cell, the cell can rupture and
          burst.
   b) They will have a tendency to gain water through osmosis,
      therefore, they must quickly get rid of excess water otherwise their
      cells will burst.
   c) They will have a tendency to lose water though osmosis so they
      must conserve water in order for their cells to work properly.

Active transport is the movement of substances against the
concentration gradient, i.e. from a low to high concentration. This
requires energy.
Villi in the small intestine. Glucose is moved by diffusion into the
body. The concentration of glucose in the villi will then become
low, so the body absorbs the remaining glucose by active
transport.

3. a) Enzymes are organic catalysts.
   b) Enzymes speed up chemical reactions in living organisms, whilst
      remaining chemically unchanged themselves.

4. a) 40°C
   b) Because it takes the least time to convert all the starch to sugar at
      this optimum temperature.
   c) None of the starch has been converted into sugar.
   d) The enzyme has been denatured by the high temperature.

5. The lock and key model is when a molecule with the correct shape
   can fit into a particular enzyme.

6 a) i)–ii) In any order.
      i) Temperature ii) pH level.
   b) The active site is changed irreversibly so that the molecule can no
      longer fit into the enzyme.

Page 9

1. 37°C

2. a)–b) In any order.
   a) Brain b) Skin.

3. The brain acts as a processing centre, receiving information from both
   the temperature receptors in the skin and the brain.

4. a)–b) In any order.
   a) Sweat glands b) Muscles.

5. If the body temperature increases, sweating occurs and the
   evaporation of the sweat removes heat energy from the skin.

6. a) i)–iv) Accept any of the following answers:
      Confusion; red or dry skin; low blood pressure; convulsions;
      fainting; rapid heartbeat.
   b) i)–ii) Accept any of the following answers:
      Remove clothes and bathe in cool water; cool body using wet
      towels or fan; place ice packs on neck, head and groin; elevate
      the legs.

Page 10

1. The hypothalamus constantly monitors temperature and switches
   various temperature controls on and off.

2. a) Vasodilation is the widening of blood vessels (capillaries) under
      the skin.
   b) The widening of the blood vessels means that more heat is lost from
      the surface of the skin by radiation, which cools the body down.

3 a) Vasoconstriction is the narrowing of blood vessels (capillaries)
      under the skin.
   b) The narrowing of the blood vessels means that less heat is lost
      from the surface of the skin by radiation, thereby conserving heat
      in the body.

4. a) 35°C
   b) i)–iv) Accept any of the following answers:
      Grey skin colour; amnesia; shivering, slurred speech, confusion;
      loss of coordination; cold skin.
   c) i)–iii) In any order. Accept any other suitable answers.
      i) Raise the core body temperature.
      ii) Insulate the body, especially the armpits, groin and head.
      iii) Give warm drinks but not alcohol.

Page 11

1. By adjusting the amount of urine that is excreted from the body.

2. b) True.
   c) False. The kidneys excrete as much salt as the body requires.
   d) True.
   e) False. The kidneys excrete the remaining urine, which is stored in
      the kidneys.

3. **a) i)–ii) Accept any of the following answers:**
   Sweating; breathing; urine production; faeces.
   b) i)–ii) Accept any of the following answers:
   Drinks; food; respiration.

4. **a)–e) In any order.**
   a) External temperature.
   b) Amount of exercise.
   c) Fluid intake.
   d) Drugs.
   e) Salt intake.

5. A diuretic increases the amount of urine produced.

6. Cells may rupture and brain damage or death may occur.

Page 12

1. Anti-diuretic hormone (ADH).

2. **a)** Receptors in the hypothalamus detect changes in salt concentration. A stimulus is sent to the pituitary gland. Thirst is stimulated to encourage drinking.
   b) Increased amount of ADH is secreted into the blood.
   c) The kidneys absorb more water.
   d) The bladder fills with a small quantity of concentrated urine.
   e) High blood water level.
   f) Receptors in the hypothalamus detect changes in salt levels.
   g) Less ADH is secreted into the blood.
   h) Kidneys absorb less water.
   i) Normal blood water level.

Page 13

1. **a)** About 100.
   b) i) A group.
   ii) Accept any other suitable answers.
   Magnesium (Mg), Calcium (Ca), Radium (Ra)
   iii) Elements in the same group have the same number of electrons in their outermost shell.
   iv) 4
   c) i) A period.
   ii) Accept any other suitable answers.
   Potassium (K), Calcium (Ca), Scandium (Sc)
   iii) They are the same.
   iv) Silver: 5 Tin: 5
   d) i) Hf
   ii) 178
   iii) 72

Page 14

1. **a)**

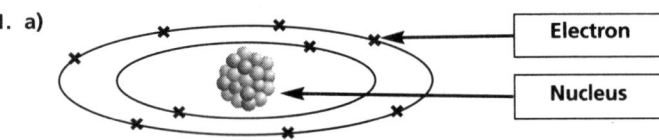

Electron

Nucleus

   b) i) +1. Positively charged.
   ii) Zero. Neutral.
   iii) -1. Negatively charged.
   iv) Zero. No electrical charge because an atom has the same number of protons as electrons.
   c) i) 1
   ii) 1
   iii) 0 (nearly). Negligible, i.e. nearly nothing, compared to a proton or neutron.

2 **a) i)** Red **ii)** Yellow **iii)** Lilac.
   b) An energy change as excited electrons fall from high energy levels to lower ones.
   c) It has helped chemists to discover new elements.

Page 15

1. **a)** Electronic configuration tells us how electrons are arranged around the nucleus of an atom in shells (energy levels).
   b) i) The first shell has a maximum of 2 electrons. The shells after that have a maximum of 8 electrons.
   ii) Potassium is in Group 1 (number of electrons in outermost shell).
   iii) It is in the fourth period (number of energy levels occupied by electrons equals the number of the period).

2 **a)** 2.8.8.2 **b)** 2.1 **c)** 2.3 **d)** 2.8.7

Page 16

1. The products of a chemical reaction are made up from exactly the same atoms as the reactants – no atoms are lost or made.

2. **a)** Nitrogen monoxide + Carbon monoxide $\longrightarrow$ Nitrogen + Carbon dioxide
   b) That two molecules of nitrogen monoxide gas and two molecules of carbon monoxide gas produce one molecule of nitrogen gas and two molecules of carbon dioxide gas.

3. **a)** $Cu + O_2 \longrightarrow CuO$
   b) Accept any suitable diagrams.
   There are 2 Os on the reactant side but only 1 O on the product side. So we need to add another CuO to the product side to balance the Os. Therefore we also need to add another Cu on the reactant side to balance the Cus.
   There are now 2 Cu atoms and 2 O atoms on each side which means the equation is balanced.
   c) $2Cu_{(s)} + O2_{(g)} \longrightarrow 2CuO_{(s)}$

Pages 17–18

1. **a)** Corrosive; they attack living tissue, including eyes and skin, and can damage materials.
   b) Oxidising; these substances provide oxygen, which allows other substances to burn more fiercely.
   c) Toxic; these substances can kill when swallowed, breathed in or absorbed through the skin.

2. **a)** Do not work near a naked flame.
   b) i)–ii) Accept any other suitable answers.
   i) Wear eye protection and gloves.
   ii) Wash hands after handling chemicals.

3. **a)** 6
   b) i) Their boiling points decrease.
   ii) They become more reactive.
   iii) Their density increases.
   c) i) Floats and melts – gentle reaction. Lithium hydroxide and hydrogen gas are formed.
   ii) Vigorous reaction to form lithium chloride.
   iii) Vigorous reaction to form sodium chloride.
   iv) Quickly tarnishes and becomes covered in a layer of potassium oxide.
   v) Floats and melts – very aggressive reaction, so much so that it catches fire. Potassium hydroxide and hydrogen gas are formed.
   vi) Vigorous reaction to form potassium chloride.

4. **a) i)** Potassium + Chlorine $\longrightarrow$ Potassium chloride
   ii) Lithium + Water $\longrightarrow$ Lithium hydroxide + Hydrogen
   iii) Sodium + Oxygen $\longrightarrow$ Sodium oxide
   b) ii) LiOH **iii)** Na_2O

5. **a)** $4M_{(s)} + O_{2(g)} = 2M_2O_{(s)}$
   b) $2M_{(s)} + 2H_2O_{(l)} = 2MOH_{(aq)} + H_{2(g)}$

6. **a) i)–iii) In any order. Accept any other suitable answers.**
   i) Use small amounts of very dilute concentrations.
   ii) Wear safety glasses and use safety screens.
   iii) Watch teacher demonstrations.
   b) Put universal indicator into a beaker of water. Universal indicator should be green to show neutral pH. Put a small piece of sodium into the beaker. Sodium reacts with water and gives off hydrogen gas. When it has finished reacting, the beaker contains sodium hydroxide solution. The solution should now be purple showing it is alkaline.

Page 19

1. **a)** 5
   b) i) Their boiling points increase.
   ii) They become less reactive.
   iii) Their densities increase.

2. **a)** A molecule that exists in pairs of atoms.
   b) i)–ii) Accept any other suitable answers.
   i) Cl_2
   ii) I_2

Lonsdale

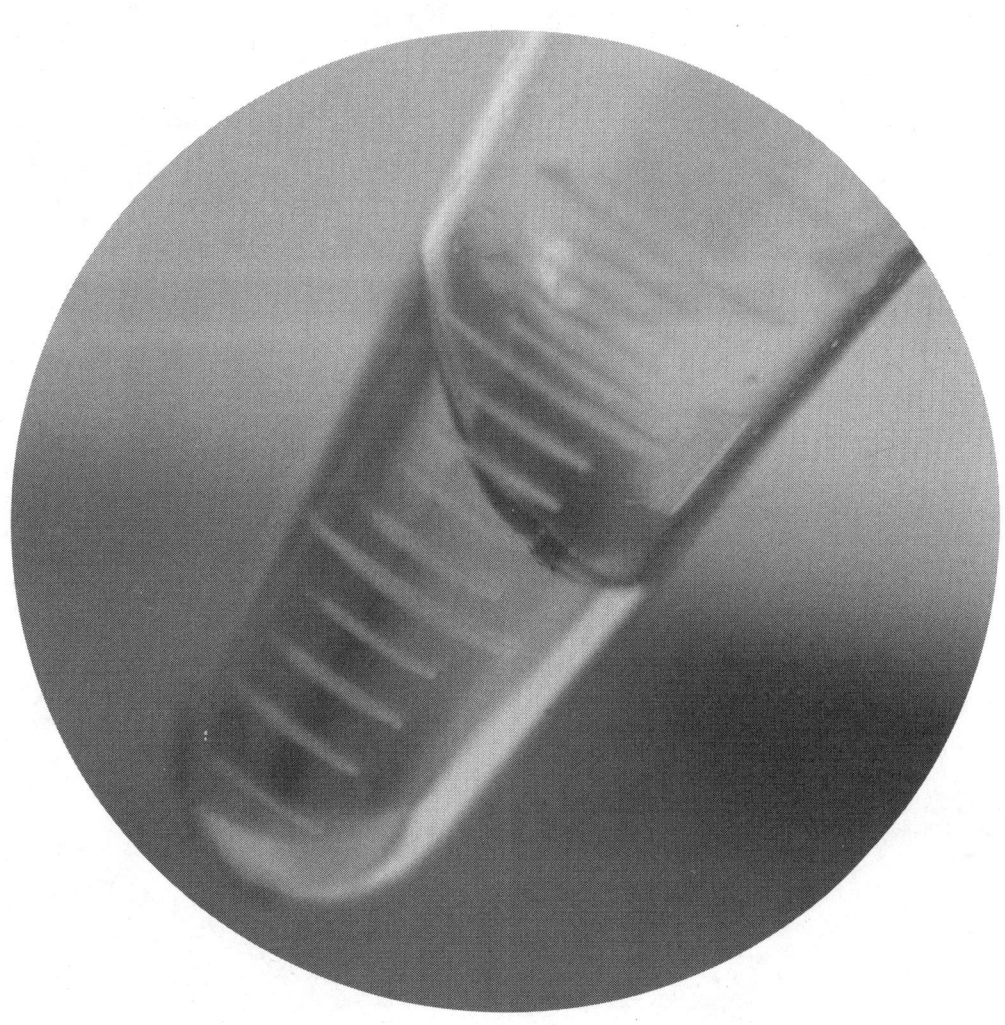

STUDENT WORKBOOK
ANSWERS

The Essentials of GCSE

OCR Additional
science

For Specification A
Dorothy Warren, Nathan Goodman, Eliot Attridge

Ordering Details

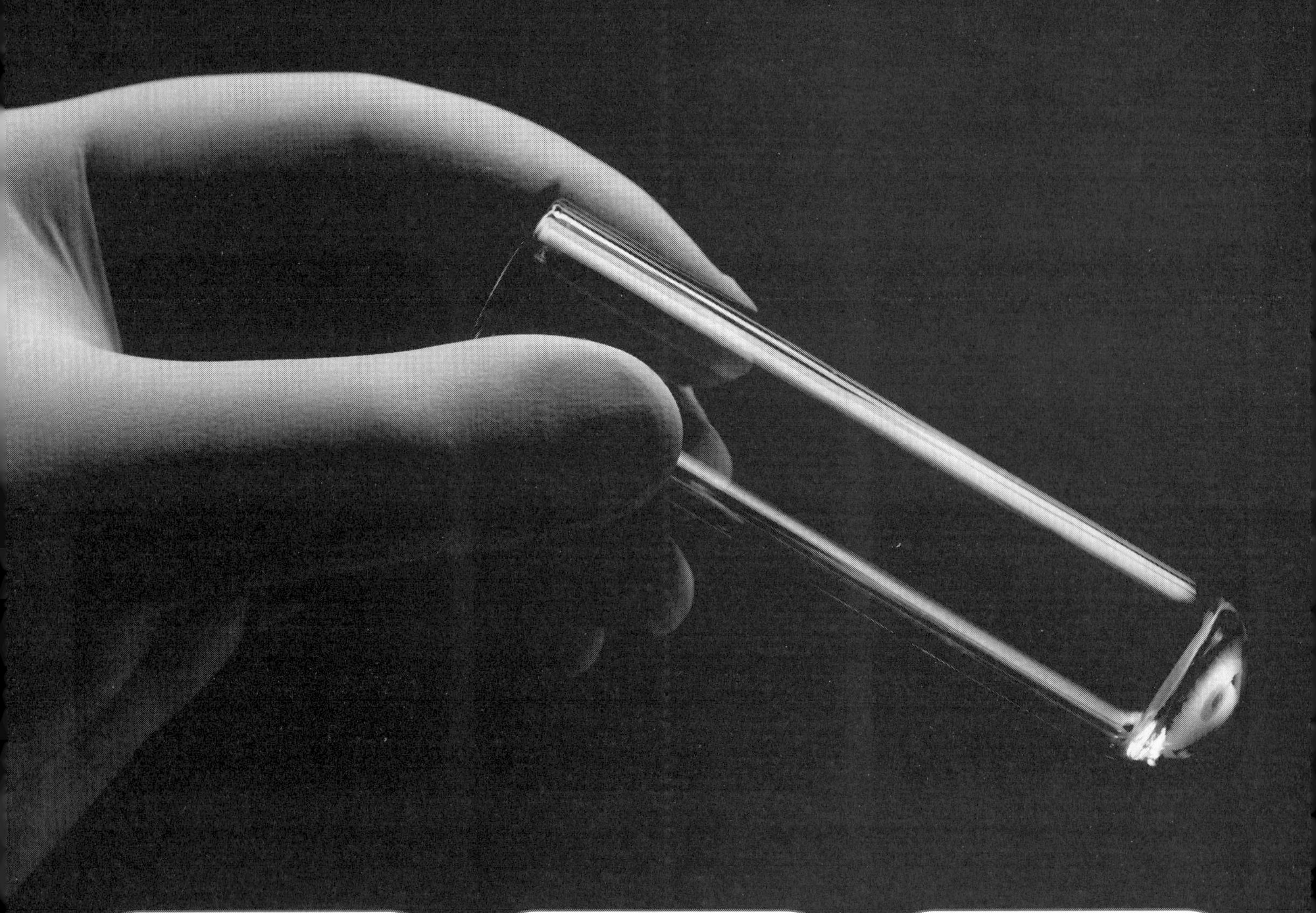

INFORMATION

For up-to-date product information, including prices, please visit our website or telephone our customer services department:

Web: www.lonsdalesrg.co.uk
Enquiries: 015395 65921

EDUCATIONAL PROVIDERS

Educational providers can order on-line and by fax, telephone or post:

Lonsdale, Westmorland House, Elmsfield Park, Holme, Carnforth Lancashire LA6 1RJ

Order Line: 015395 65920
Fax: 015395 64167
Web: www.lonsdalesrg.co.uk

PRIVATE CUSTOMERS

Secure ordering is available on-line at **www.lonsdalesrg.co.uk**

3. a) Sterilising water, making pesticides and plastics **b)** HCl **c)** NaCl **d)** Orange liquid **e)** HBr **f)** NaBr **g)** Grey solid **h)** Antiseptic to sterilise wounds **i)** NaI

4. Displacement reaction.

Page 20

1. a) They have the same number of electrons in their outermost shell. In Group 1, the highest occupied energy level contains 1 electron. In Group 7, the highest occupied energy level contains 7 electrons.
   b) The outermost electron shell gets further away from the influence of the nucleus and so an electron is more easily lost.
   c) The outermost electron shell gets further away from the influence of the nucleus and so an electron is less easily gained.

2. a) Negative and positive electrodes are placed in a electrolyte solution. A power supply is connected to the electrodes and the positive particles are attracted to the negative electrodes whilst the negative particles are attracted to the positive electrode.
   b) Ions

3. a) An ion is formed when an atom loses or gains one or more electrons and it carries an overall charge because the proton and electron numbers are no longer equal.
   b) A cation is when an ion has been formed by an atom losing an electron(s) and it has an overall positive charge, because it now has more protons than electrons.
   An anion is when an ion has been formed by an atom gaining an electron(s), and it has an overall negative charge, because it now has more electrons than protons.

Pages 21–22

1. Group 1 and Group 7

2. The K atom has 1 electron in its outer shell which is transferred to the chlorine atom, so they both have 8 electrons in their outer shell. The atoms become K^+ and Cl^- and the compound formed is potassium chloride or KCl.

3. A giant crystal lattice

4.

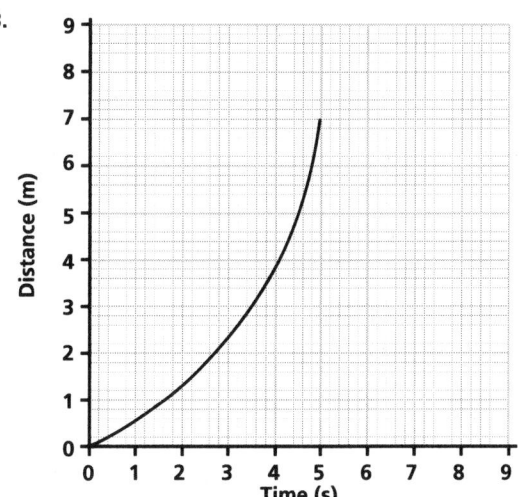

5. The Ca atom has 2 electrons in its outer shell which is transferred to the O atom, so they both have 8 electrons in their outer shell. The atoms become Ca^{2+} and O^{2-}, and the compound formed is calcium oxide, CaO.

6. There is a strong force of attraction between the ions, which takes a lot of energy to break, leading to high melting and boiling points. When the compound is molten or dissolved, the charged ions are free to move around the liquid, so they can conduct electricity.

7. a) i) LiOH **ii)** 2LiO **iii)** Al_2O_3
   b) i) 2^+ **ii)** 2^+ **iii)** 6^+

Pages 23–24

1. Speed is the distance an object travels in a given time. Velocity is the object's speed and the direction.

2. -10m/s

3. a) 15m **b)** 5m

4. Speed = Distance / Time

5. i) 10m/s **ii)** 5m/s **iii)** 100m **iv)** 600m **v)** 3s **vi)** 10s

6. Average speed calculates the total distance travelled even if the speed is not constant. Instantaneous speed is the speed at a particular point.

7. a) 4m/s **b)** 0m/s **c)** 4m/s **d)** 20m/s **e)** 10s **f)** 2m/s

8. a) 30mph **b)** 15mph

9. a)

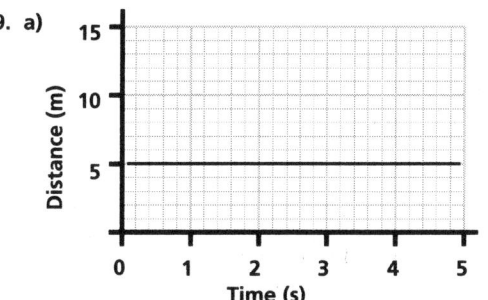

b)

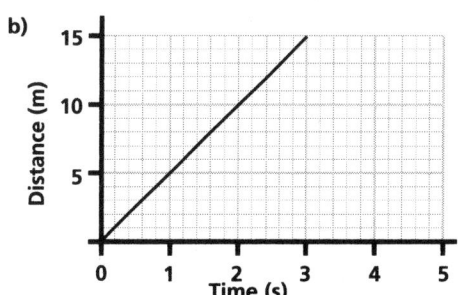

Page 25

1. a) 0 **b)** 1.3m/s

2. It indicates that the object is speeding up.

3.

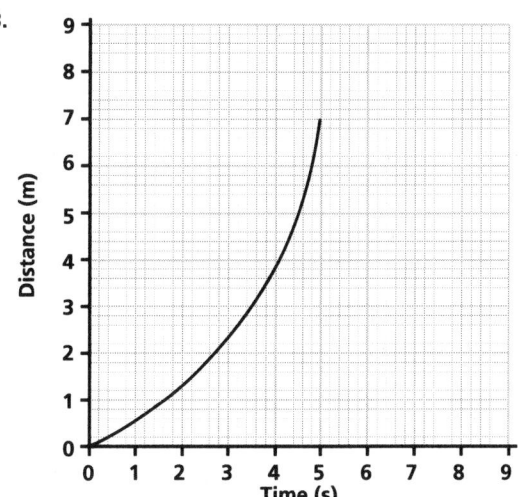

4.

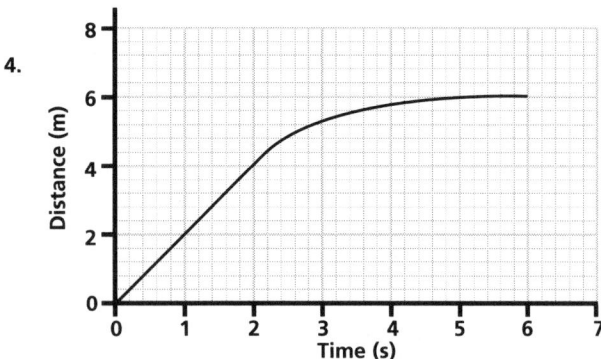

Page 26

1. The slope of a velocity–time graph represents how quickly an object is increasing in speed.

2. **a)**

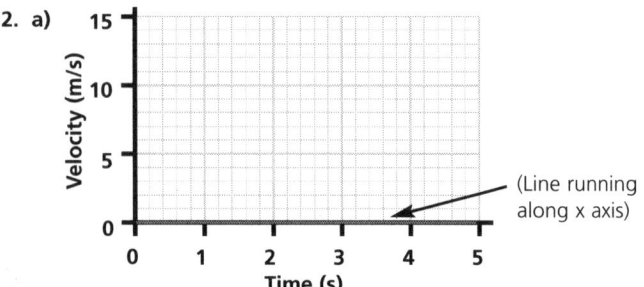

(Line running along x axis)

b)

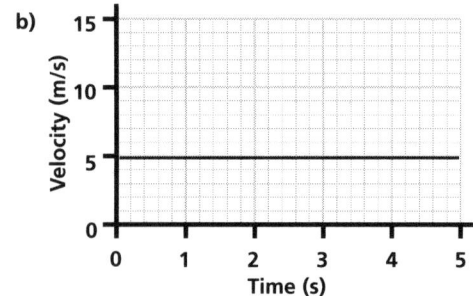

c)

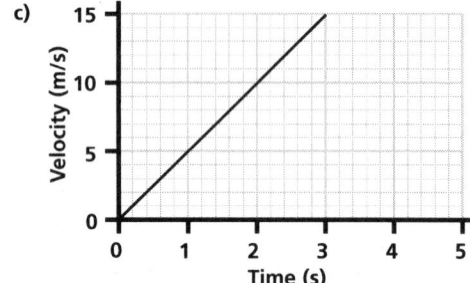

d)

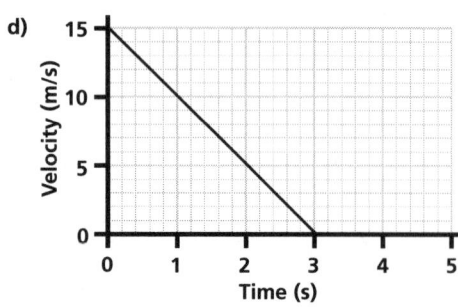

3. The lorry accelerates for 2 seconds; velocity increases by 5m/s. Then the lorry travels at a constant velocity for 2 seconds. Finally, it decelerates for 1 second; velocity decreases by 10m/s.

Pages 27–28

1. A force occurs when two objects interact with each other.

2. **a)** Friction
   b) Acts to slow a falling object down.
   c) Reaction of the surface.
   d) Attracts two masses towards each other.

3. A jet engine pushes gas backwards (action) and the gas pushes the engine forwards (reaction) moving the object through the air.

4. The sum of all the forces acting on an object.

5. **a)** ⟶ 300N. Car will speed up.
   b) ⟵ 2000N. Car will slow down and stop.
   c) 0N. Car will continue at the same speed.

6. Friction and reaction occur as a response to another force.

7. An object resting on a surface is pulled down to the surface by gravity. The surface pushes up with an equal and opposite force called reaction of the surface.

8. c

9. d

10. a

11. c

12. c

Page 29

1. **a)–b) In any order.**
   a) Mass **b)** Velocity

2. **a)** 500kg m/s **b)** 30 000kg m/s **c)** 100kg **d)** 400kg **e)** 2kg
   f) 1000kg

3. **a)–b) In any order.**
   a) The size of the resultant force.
   b) The length of time the force is acting on the object.

4. **a)** 30 000kg m/s **b)** 10 000kg m/s **c)** 20 000kg m/s **d)** 20m/s

5. 0

6. 15m/s

Pages 30–32

1. **a)** They would experience a greater momentum.
   b) They would experience a larger force.

2. The crumple zone reduces the momentum of the car which means that the force exerted on the people inside the car will be reduced, which will result in fewer injuries.

3. **a)** 1500kg m/s
   b) 0kg m/s
   c) 1500kg m/s
   d) 15 000N

4. **a)** True **b)** True **c)** False **d)** True **e)** False

5. The kinetic energy is transformed to other forms of energy, i.e. heat energy on the car's brakes.

6. 350J

7. **a)** Gravitational potential energy is the energy gained by an object when it is lifted off the ground.
   b) 500J
   c) Its gravitational energy decreases and is converted to kinetic energy.

8. 10J

9. Energy; loses; gains

10. 60 000J

11. 1 000 000 000J

12. **a)** 1 000 000J
    b) 1 000 000J
    c) Air resistance.
    d) 200m/s

Page 33

1. **a)** DNA determines the biological development of all cellular life forms.
   b) iv

2. **a)** Cellulose **b)** Nucleus **c)** Cell membrane **d)** Ribosome
   e) Permanent vacuole

3. Mitosis is the process by which a cell divides into two 'daughter' cells, which are genetically identical to both each other and to the parent cell.

4. **a)–b) In any order.**
   a) The number of organelles increases.
   b) The chromosomes are copied.

5. If they were not copied, the daughter cells would be incomplete and could not function.

6. **a)** Mitosis and meiosis **b)** Mitosis **c)** Mitosis **d)** Meiosis **e)** Mitosis

Page 34

1. Fertilisation is when the nuclei of a male gamete (sperm) and a female gamete (egg) fuse together.

2. A zygote.

3. It is important that both the sperm and egg cells only have half the number of chromosomes as the parent cell, so when they fuse together they can produce a new cell body with new pairs of chromosomes.

4. Chromosome; father or mother; mother or father; cells; meiosis; chromosomes; cell.

5. Bone, muscle and nerve cells.

6. 100 trillion.

7. Because only one allele from each parent is passed onto the offspring so the characteristics will be different to those of the parents.

8. **Accept any suitable diagram.**

Page 35

1. Genes provide instructions for the production of proteins and therefore control the development of the organism, and any characteristics such as the ability to roll your tongue.

2. **a) i)–iv) In any order.**
   i) Adenine **ii)** Thymine **iii)** Cytosine **iv)** Guanine
   b) i)–ii) In any order.
   i) Adenine pairs up with Thymine.
   ii) Cytosine pairs up with Guanine.
   c) Accept any suitable diagram.

3. The DNA is unzipped. Relevant genes are copied into smaller molecules called messenger RNA (mRNA). The mRNA is read by ribosomes and proteins are made.

4. 20

5. It is dependent upon the amino acids that make it up.

Page 36

1. Mitosis

2. At the 16-cell stage, approximately 4 days after fertilisation.

3. **a)–b) In any order.**
   a) Their position relative to one another.
   b) The distribution of proteins within the cell is different.

4. Only those needed by that cell.

5. 20 000 to 25 000

6. **a)–c) In any order.**
   a) Embryos **b)** Blood from the umbilical cord **c)** Adult cells

7. Therapeutic cloning is the process which involves removing the nucleus from an egg cell and replacing it with a nucleus from one of the patient's cells. The egg is then stimulated so that it starts to divide.

8 **a)** The problem with using adult stem cells is that they only produce a certain type of cell, rather than any type of cell like embryonic stem cells.
   b) The advantage of using adult stem cells is that they have been taken from the patient so the patient's immune system will not reject the transplant.

Page 37

1. Unlike animals, most plant cells continue to grow in height and width throughout their lives.

2. **a)** It is the location of plant growth where unspecialised cells divide repeatedly.
   b) They can develop into any type of plant cell.
   c) i) Width of the plant.
   ii) Height and root length.
   d) Accept any suitable drawings.

3. **a)** A callus is a cluster of undifferentiated cells containing the same genetic information as the parent.
   b) It can be created when cells from the meristem are grown in a special culture medium.
   c) By adding special plant hormones.

Pages 38–39

1. They are used by the plant to transport water and soluble mineral salts from the roots to the leaves.

2. Phloem tubes are used by the plant to transport dissolved food to the whole plant for respiration or storage.

3. Cuttings are taken from the parent plant. The cuttings are dipped into a rooting hormone and then planted into soil or a growing medium. Roots will develop and a new plant will grow which will be an identical copy of the parent plant.

4. **a)** A plant needs to be able to respond to light to photosynthesise and therefore grow and survive.
   b) Phototropism.

5. **Accept any suitable drawing which shows the seedlings growing in the direction of the light source at the side of the box.**

6. **a)** Auxins
   b) They affect cell division at the tip of a shoot and cause the cells to elongate (become longer).

7. The light source hits the shoot from the left. The concentration of auxins in the side of the shoot closest to the light decreases and the cells do not grow very quickly. The concentration of auxins in the side of the shoot furthest away from the light increases and, therefore, the cells grow quickly and the shoot begins to bend towards the light.

8. **a)** The shoot will grow straight upwards towards the source of the light.
   b) The auxins control the growth of the shoot, so without them the cells cannot grow. There will be no growth.
   c) The covered shoot is stimulated to produce extra auxins but is unable to detect the light so it will grow straight up.
   d) The foil covering in this position does not affect the growth of the auxins so the shoot will grow in the direction of the light source, i.e. it will bend over towards the left.

Page 40

1. **a)** Biosphere **b)** Atmosphere **c) i)** Hydrosphere **ii)** Lithosphere

I	A	B	L	E	S	U	T	F	O	W	T	M
C	W	G	X	C	S	L	G	A	N	H	N	E
O	A	S	A	M	E	A	V	G	Y	T	M	L
M	T	V	O	B	R	E	W	D	R	E	P	E
P	M	T	Y	I	T	T	R	S	O	R	E	V
O	O	I	L	O	I	O	T	L	D	F	C	V
U	S	H	U	S	S	N	C	A	X	C	V	P
N	P	B	K	P	E	D	P	C	Z	B	N	Y
D	H	F	H	H	U	R	N	I	Q	W	L	O
S	E	E	E	E	D	F	R	M	C	X	Z	A
R	R	F	Y	R	P	G	S	E	T	Y	E	C
E	E	R	Y	E	G	A	S	H	R	J	K	L
I	L	I	T	H	O	S	P	H	E	R	E	S
P	R	O	P	E	R	T	I	E	S	T	W	Y

2. a)–c) In any order.
    a) Silicon, (Si) b) Oxygen, (O) c) Aluminium, (Al)

3. a)–d) In any order.
    a) Carbon, (C) b) Hydrogen, (H) c) Oxygen, (O) d) Nitrogen, (N)

Page 41

1. a)–b) In any order.
    a) Nitrogen b) Carbon

2. The carbon cycle is the continual recycling of carbon in nature. For example carbon dioxide is moved by green plants during photosynthesis, into the biosphere, and is then returned to the atmosphere during respiration.

3. a) Lithosphere
    b) Nitrogen is returned to the lithosphere.
    c) By denitrifying bacteria.

4. Burning fossil fuels.

Page 42

1. a)–e) In any order.
    a) Oxygen b) Nitrogen c) Carbon dioxide d) Water vapour
    e) Argon

2. a) It tells us that they are gases.
    b) They are small molecules with weak forces of attraction between them. Only small amounts of energy are needed to break these forces, which allow the molecules to move freely through the air.
    c) No charge – when pure they do not conduct electricity.
    d) i) They are connected by strong covalent bonds.
       ii) There is an electrostatic attraction between the nuclei of the atoms and the shared pair of electrons. **Accept any suitable diagram showing shared electrons between the nuclei.**

Pages 43–44

1. It contains dissolved ionic compounds called 'salts'.

2. a)–c) In any order. Accept any other suitable answers.
    a) Sodium chloride.
    b) Magnesium sulfate.
    c) Potassium chloride.

3. It has a much higher boiling point than all of the other small molecules in the hydrosphere.

4. It is bent, because the electrons in the covalent bond are nearer the oxygen atom than the hydrogen atoms. There are small charges on the atoms which mean that the forces between the molecules are slightly stronger than in other covalent molecules. More energy is therefore needed to separate them.

5. The small charges on the atoms. They attract the charges on the ions; the ions can then break away and move freely through the liquid.

6. a) Silicon dioxide.

    b) i)–iv) In any order.
    i) Very hard ii) High melting and boiling points iii) Electrical insulator iv) Insoluble in water

7. a)–b) In any order.
    a) Quartz b) Sandstone

8. a) There are no free electrons or ions to carry the electrical charge.
    b) A lot of energy is needed to break the strong covalent bond between the atoms.

9. a)–c) In any order.
    a) Carbohydrates b) Proteins c) DNA

10. Glucose contains carbon, hydrogen and oxygen.

11. a) Fat 2 b) DNA c) Protein

Page 45

1. The mass of the reactants is equal to the mass of the products, so there are the same numbers of atoms on both sides of the equation.

b) i)–ii) In any order.
    i) Write a number in front of one or more of the formulae. This increases the number of all of the atoms in the formula.
    ii) Remember to include the state symbols.

2. a) $Cu_{(s)} + O_{2(g)} \longrightarrow CuO_{(s)}$
    b) Because there are more oxygen atoms on the reactants side.
    c) $2Cu_{(s)} + O_{2(g)} \longrightarrow 2CuO_{(s)}$

3. a) It is a number that compares the mass of one atom to the mass of other atoms.
    b) A_r
    c) i) The larger of the two (at the top of the symbol).
       ii) The mass number.

Page 46

1. a) Minerals
    b) A rock that contains varying amounts of minerals from which metals can be extracted.

2. a) They are very reactive metals and so energy is required to extract them from their ores.
    b) Electrolysis
    c) i) Carbon
       ii) They are extracted by heating with carbon / carbon monoxide.
    d) i)–ii) In any order.
       i) Gold ii) Platinum

3. a) In 100g of CuO there will be $\frac{63.5}{79.5}$ x 100 = 79.9g of Cu
    b) Relative formula mass: (2 x 79.5) + 12 = (2 x 63.5) + 44
                                      159 + 12 = 127 + 44
                                           171 = 171
    Therefore, 159g of CuO produces 127g of Cu

    So, 1g of CuO = $\frac{127}{159}$ = 0.8g of Cu

Page 47

1. a) A life cycle analysis.
    b) i) Extraction ii) Use iii) Disposal

2. a) i)–ii) In any order.
       i) Energy use ii) Transport
    b) i)–iii) In any order.
       i) Reuse ii) Recycle iii) Throw away

3. a) The decomposition of an electrolyte (solution that conducts electricity) with an electric current.
    b) In industry to extract metals from their ores.

4. The ions have to be free to move – this happens when it is either molten or dissolved in solution.

5. The positively charged ions (in this case, lead) are attracted to the negative electrode. The negatively charged ions (bromide) are attracted to the positive electrode.

6. a) Discharged.

    b) It means that the ions lose their charge.

Page 48

1. a) It is too reactive to be extracted by heating with carbon.
    b) Purified aluminium oxide and cryolite (a compound of aluminium) to lower its melting point.
    c) It is melted.
    d) i) The positively charged aluminium ions move towards the negative cathode and aluminium is formed.
       ii) Negatively charged oxygen ions move towards the positive electrode and oxygen is formed.
    e) Large amounts of electrical energy are needed to carry out the extraction and this is expensive.
    f) $2Al_2O_{3(l)} \longrightarrow 4Al_{(l)} + 3O_{2(g)}$
    g) $Al^{3+}_{(l)} + 3e^- \xrightarrow{\text{reduction}} Al_{(l)}$
    h) $2O^{2-}_{(l)} - 4e^- \xrightarrow{\text{oxidation}} O_{2(g)}$

Page 49

1. a) i)–iv) In any order.
    i) Strong ii) Malleable iii) High melting point iv) Conduct electricity

b) i)–iv) In any order.
  i) Strong. Metal ions are closely packed in a lattice structure.
  ii) Malleable. External forces cause layers of metal ions to move by sliding over other layers.
  iii) High melting point. A lot of energy is needed to break the strong force of attraction between the metal ions and the sea of electrons.
  iv) Conduct electricity. Electrons are free to move throughout the structure. When an electrical force is applied the electrons move along the metal in one direction.

c) Accept any other suitable answers.
  i) Conducts heat ii) Electrical switches iii) Iron iv) High melting point
  v) Aluminium vi) Malleable vii) Lightweight viii) Lightweight
  ix) Bicycles x) Submarines

Page 50

1. Electrical charge; insulating; negative; negatively; positively; lose electrons

2. a) i b) iii c) ii d) ii e) i

3. The car panel is positively charged, and the paint is negatively charged. The paint particles repel each other but are attracted to the positively charged panel and this causes the paint to be applied evenly.

Page 51

1 a) An electric current is a flow of charge.
  b) Amperes

2. Metals contain free electrons and the movement of these electrons create the flow of charge.

3. a)

  b) Battery
  c)

  d)
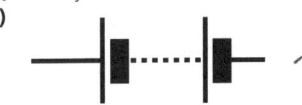

  e) Glows when current flows though a circuit.
  f) Ammeter
  g) Measures current.
  h) Voltmeter
  i) Measures potential difference (voltage).
  j)
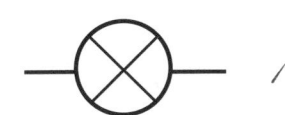

  k) Allows current to flow through a circuit.
  l) Fixed resistor.
  m)

4. Direct current flows in one direction only. Alternating current continuously changes direction.

5. It depends on the resistance of the components in the circuit and the potential difference across them.

6. Potential difference is the measure of the 'push' of the battery on the charges in a circuit.

4. The greater the potential difference across a component, the greater the current that flows through the component.

Page 52

1. The resistance of a component is how much a component stops the flow of charge.

2. a) Adding resistors in series increases the total resistance.
  b) Adding resistors in parallel reduces the total resistance.

3. When an electric current flows through a component, the component heats up. If the current is large enough the wire in a component could get so hot that it could melt.

4. a) 10 ohms b) 4 ohms c) 21.3 ohms d) 2.5 ohms e) 2.7 ohms

5. a) 150 ohms b) 36 ohms c) 0.4A d) 0.3A

Pages 53–54

1.
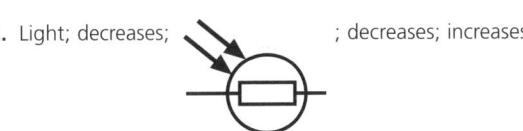

2. Light; decreases; 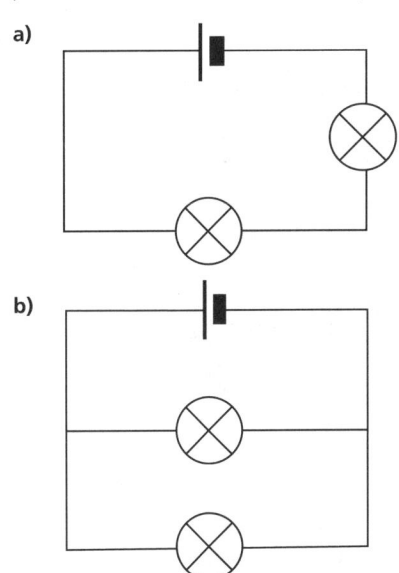 ; decreases; increases

3. a) The potential difference remains the same.
  b) The current remains the same.

4. In a series circuit there is only one path for the current to take; in a parallel circuit there is more than one path for the current to take.

5. a)

  b)

6. **Resistor A:** 1 ohm
  Resistor B: 2 ohm

7. The amount of current which passes though a component depends on the resistance of the component. The greater the resistance the smaller the current will be. Therefore, a greater current will flow through a component which has a lower resistance.

8. a) 2A b) 3V c) 1V d) 4A, 4A e) 1A, 4A

9. The resistor with a larger resistance will end up with a greater share of potential difference because it takes more energy to push the current through the resistor.

Page 55

1. a)–b) In any order.
  a) By moving the magnet out of the coil.
  b) By moving the other pole of the magnet into the coil.

2. a) No current would flow.
  b) If there is no movement of the coil or magnet, the magnetic field is not being cut and, therefore, there is no induced current.

3. If a coil was rotating around a fixed magnet, the coil would become twisted. A commutator with brush contacts would need to be used, but brush contacts wear down with time and would need replacing, so there would be high maintenance costs.

4. a)–c) Accept any three from the following: increasing the speed of rotation of the magnet; increasing the strength of the magnetic field; increasing the number of turns on the coil; placing an iron core inside the coil.

5. a) During each revolution, the magnetic field is cut and the induced voltage across the coil changes its direction of flow.
   b) Alternating current.

Page 56

1. It is the amount of energy that is transferred every second.

2. a) Power = Potential difference x Current
   b) 2200W
   c) 550W

3. 13.6A

4. They are used to change the voltage of alternating current.

5. a) 100 turns **b)** 100V **c)** 1:20

Page 57

1. a) ii **b)** i **c)** iii

2. 3600J   Joule cap   W/s.

3. 1.5kWh

4. 12.5p

5. a) 80% **b)** 10% **c)** 200J

Pages 58–59

1. Stimuli; conditions; survival; responses; central nervous system.

2. c, f, e, a, d, g, b

3. a) The central nervous system (brain and spinal cord) coordinates mammals' responses and allows them to react to their surroundings.
   b) The peripheral nervous system transmits messages all over the body via sensory and motor neurons.

4. Accept any suitable diagrams.
   Sensory neurons carry electrical impulses from receptors towards the cell body and the central nervous system. Motor neurons carry electrical impulses away from the cell body and the central nervous system towards effectors.

5. A receptor responds to stimuli in the environment and passes on information, in the form of electrical impulses, to the central nervous system.

6. An effector receives information from the central nervous system and responds to it.

7. b) Smell **c)** Sound **d)** Touch **e)** Taste

8. Step 1: Impulses travel along motor neurons and terminate at the muscle cells.
   Step 2: The impulses cause the muscle cells to contract.

9. When light enters the eye it passes through the lens which focuses the light onto light-sensitive cells in the retina. The receptor cells respond to the stimuli and send impulses along sensory neurons to the brain.

10. The hormone-secreting glands are effectors, and the signal sent from the central nervous system triggers the release of the hormone into the bloodstream where it is transported to wherever it is needed.

Page 60

1. a) Neurons are specially adapted cells that carry an electrical signal when stimulated.
   b) In order to make connections from one part of the body to another.
   c) To enable a neuron to interact with many other neurons or effectors.

2. A long fibre of cytoplasm surrounded by a cell membrane.

3. To insulate the cell from the signals travelling along other neurons, and increase the speed at which the nerve impulse is transmitted.

4. a) A synapse is the gap between adjacent neurons. They allow the brain to form interconnected neural circuits.
   b) Between 100 to 500 trillion.
   c) The number of synapses decreases with age so children will have more synapses than adults.

5. c, a, d, b

Pages 61–63

1. a) It is a fast, automatic, involuntary response.
   b) i) A = Sensory neuron, B = Relay neuron, C = Motor neuron, D = Receptor
      ii) A receptor is stimulated by pain, causing impulses to pass along a sensory neuron into the spinal cord. The sensory neuron synapses with a relay neuron, by-passing the brain. The relay neuron synapses with a motor neuron sending impulses to effector muscles in the arm which contract causing the hand to be pulled quickly away.

2. Simple reflex actions mean that animals will automatically respond to a stimulus in a way that helps it to survive, e.g. by finding food, avoiding injury etc.

3 a) i)–ii) In any order. Accept any other suitable answers.
   i) Grasping reflex – tightly grasping a finger that is placed in its hand.
   ii) Startled reflex – shooting out arms and legs when startled.
   b) That their nervous system is not developing properly.

4. a) If there is little light, the radial muscles contract and the circular muscles relax which increases the size of the pupil in order to let more light in.
   b) If the light is very bright the radial muscles relax and the circular muscles contract which decreases the size of the pupil in order to let less light in.

5. a) Conditioning
   b) i) The stimulus that naturally triggers the response (the primary stimulus).
      ii) The new stimulus which triggers the response (the secondary stimulus).
   c) A Russian scientist named Pavlov.
   d) i) Meat is produced and the smell causes the dog to salivate.
      ii) The bell is repeatedly rung when meat is given to the dog. The dog starts to associate the sound of the bell with the smell of meat.
      iii) Just ringing the bell is enough to cause the dog to salivate whether meat is present or not.

6. a) The cinnabar caterpillar is brightly coloured to warn predators that it is poisonous.
   b) After birds have eaten a few of the caterpillars they associate the bright colours with an unpleasant taste and do not eat any more. Although individual caterpillars may still be eaten, the species as a whole has a better chance of survival.

7. a) A reflex action takes place which causes the hand to pull back rapidly.
   b) The brain would have to send an override signal, via a neuron, to modify the response of the reflex so the plate is not dropped.

Page 64

1. a

2. Accept any suitable answer.

3. In the first few years after birth.

4. a) They become stimulated every time an individual has a new experience.
   b) They are eventually deleted.

5. a) Everytime an experience is repeated the neuron pathways are strengthened. These pathways are more likely to transmit impulses and an individual will become better at a given task.

b) i)–iii) In any order. Accept any other suitable answers.
  i) Riding a bicycle ii) Revising for an exam iii) Learning to ski.

6. Plasticity is the brain's ability to strengthen and retain, or delete, neuron pathways throughout its lifetime.

7. A PET scan shows the level of neuron activity in different parts of the brain in response to learning words through speaking, hearing and seeing them.

Page 65

1. **a) i)–ii) In any order. Accept any other suitable answers.**
    i) Being deliberately isolated, i.e. being kept in a cellar.
    ii) Being accidentally isolated, e.g. through being shipwrecked.
   b) Genie will have had no social interaction and will therefore not have gained, or will have lost, the ability to talk.

2. **a) i)–ii) In any order. Accept any other suitable answers.**
    i) Able to lift their heads when placed on someone's shoulder.
    ii) Able to grasp a rattle when it is given to them.
   b) i)–ii) In any order. Accept any other suitable answers.
    i) Able to hold a cup and drink from it.
    ii) Walk when one hand is held.
   c) It could mean that there are neurological problems or they are lacking any necessary stimulation.

3. **a) i)–ii) In any order. Accept any other suitable answers.**
    i) Follow spoken commands.
    ii) Sniff out drugs and explosives.
   b) i)–ii) In any order. Accept any other suitable answers.
    i) Collect food from a person's hand.
    ii) Push underwater buttons to release food.

Pages 66–67

1. **a)–d) In any order**
   a) Intelligence **b)** Memory **c)** Language **d)** Consciousness

2. The physiological technique is where the effects of illness and accidents on the brain are studied in order to understand which parts of the brain control different functions.

3. **a)–b) In any order.**
   a) EEG (electroencephalogram). This is a visual record of the electrical activity of the brain measured by placing electrodes on the scalp and tracing the rise and fall of electrical potentials called brain waves.
   b) MRI (Magnetic Resonance Imaging) scanning. A scan creates computer-generated images which uses colour to represent different levels of electrical activity in the brain.

4. Store; retrieve; short-term memory; long-term memory; information; unlimited.

5. **a)** 7 (plus or minus 2)
   b) By dividing the information into chunks of groups of 3.
   c) i) 026 485 760 947 **ii)** 623 609 580 905 114

6. **a)** Drugs can cause changes in the speeds at which nerve impulses travel to the brain, speeding them up or slowing them down. Sometimes false signals can be sent.
   b) i) Alcohol causes nerve impulses to be sent slower.
    ii) Caffeine causes nerve impulses to be sent faster.

7. **a)–c) In any order.**
   a) If there is a pattern to it, or if a pattern can be imposed on it.
   b) If the information is repeated, especially over an extended period of time.
   c) If there is a strong stimulus associated with the information, e.g. colour, light, smell etc.

8. Ecstasy blocks the sites in the brain synapses where serotonin (the chemical associated with feeling happy) is released. The serotonin concentrations increase and the user experiences a feeling of elation.

9. The neurons are harmed in the process and this can lead to memory loss.

Pages 68–69

1. **a)–e) In any order. Accept any other suitable answers.**
   a) Pharmaceuticals **b)** Cosmetics **c)** Fertilisers **d)** Paints
   e) Industrial glass

2. **a)** Bulk chemicals.
   b) i)–ii) In any order.
    i) Sulfuric acid ii) Ammonia

3. **a)** A small scale.
   b) i)–ii) In any order.
    i) Drugs ii) Pesticides
   c) Because many of them can be hazardous and you need to learn about the necessary precautions that should be taken.

4. **a)** A measure of the acidity or alkalinity of an aqueous solution across a 14-point scale.
   b) i) An acid is a substance that has a pH of less than 7.
    ii) An alkali is a soluble base (a base being the oxides and hydroxides of metals) that has a pH of more than 7.

5. **a) i)** Neutral **ii)** Very acidic **iii)** Very alkaline **iv)** Slightly acidic
    v) Slightly alkaline
   b) i)–iii) Accept any other suitable answers.
    i) Hydrochloric acid ii) Water iii) Dilute sodium hydroxide
   c) It is measured using an indicator such as universal indicator solution or a pH meter.

6. **a) i)** Sodium hydroxide **ii)** Alkali
   b) i) Sulfuric acid **ii)** Acid
   c) i) Calcium hydroxide **ii)** Alkali
   d) i) Hydrochloric acid (hydrogen chloride) **ii)** Acid
   e) i) Potassium hydroxide **ii)** Alkali

7. **a)** Aqueous hydrogen ions ($H^+_{(aq)}$)
   b) Aqueous hydroxide ions ($OH^-_{(aq)}$)

Page 70

1. **a)** Neutralisation is where an acid and a base are mixed together in the correct amounts and 'cancel' each other out.
   b) 7
   c) Acid + Base $\longrightarrow$ Neutral salt solution + Water
   d) $H^+_{(aq)} + OH^-_{(aq)} \longrightarrow H_2O_{(l)}$

2. **a) i)–ii) In any order.**
    i) The metal in the base ii) The acid used
   b) i) Chloride salts **ii)** Sulfate salts **iii)** Nitrate salts

3. **a)** Copper sulfate.
   b) $NaCl_{(aq)}$
   c) Potassium nitrate
   d) $Ca(NO_3)_{2(aq)}$

Pages 71–72

1. **a i)–iii) In any order.**
    i) $NaCl$ ii) KCl iii) Na_2CO_3
   b) i) Na = 1+, Cl = 1-
    ii) K = 1+, Cl = 1-
    iii) Na_2 = 2+, CO_3 = 2-

2. **a) i)–iii) In any order. Accept any other suitable answers.**
    i) $MgSO_4$ ii) $MgCO_3$ iii) $CaCl_2$
   b) Answers included for salts listed above. Accept correct answers for other suitable salts.
    i) Mg = 2+, SO_4 = 2-
    ii) Mg = 2+, CO_3 = 2-
    iii) Ca = 2+, Cl_2 = 2-

3. **a)–d) In any order.**
   a) Chlorine, Cl_2 **b)** Hydrogen, H_2 **c)** Nitrogen, N_2 **d)** Oxygen, O_2

4. **a)** More of it is formed.
   b) Percentage yield = $\dfrac{\text{Actual yield}}{\text{Theoretical yield}} \times 100$

5. **i) Answer given ii)** Risk assessment **iii)** Temperature **iv)** Product **v)** Purify **vi)** Yield **vii)** Purity.

6. **a)** Zinc + Hydrochloric acid $\longrightarrow$ Zinc chloride + Hydrogen
   b) Wear safety glasses; zinc chloride is corrosive so it is harmful if inhaled or swallowed. Do not allow it to come in contact with your skin; wear protective gloves. Ensure that there is adequate ventilation.
   c) Filter it using a paper filter and a funnel.
   d) 10%

Page 73

1. **a)–c) Accept any three from the following:** relative atomic mass; relative formula mass; that a balanced equation shows the number of atoms / molecules taking part in the reaction; how to work out the ratio of mass of reactant to mass of product; how to apply the ratio to the question.

2. **a) i)** 27 **ii)** 35 **iii)** 14 **iv)** 40 **v)** 73
   b) The mass number.

3. **a) i)** The relative atomic masses of all its elements added together.
   ii) M_r
   b) i)–ii) In any order.
   i) Formula of the compound.
   ii) Relative atomic mass of all the atoms involved.
   c) i) 159 **ii)** 98 **iii)** 17

Page 74

1. **a) i)** 100 **ii)** 72 **iii)** 110 **iv)** 44 **v)** 18
   b) 172
   c) 172
   d) Yes. There is no loss of mass in a chemical reaction.
   e) 2.2g

2. 0.91kg / 909g

Page 75

1. **a)** Titrations can be used to calculate the purity of an acid by neutralising the acid with a known amount of alkali.
   b) i) Burette, alkali.
   ii) Distilled water.
   iii) Pipette, acid.
   iv) Indicator, colourless, burette.
   v) Alkali, burette.
   vi) Repeat, same.

2. Divide by 1000.

3. **a)** 3 x the volume and concentration of the alkali divided by the volume of citric acid.
   b) Mass = Concentration x Value
   c) $\dfrac{\text{Calculated mass}}{\text{Mass weighed out at start}} \times 100$

Page 76

1. **a)** They collide with each other with sufficient energy to react.
   b) i)–ii) Accept any other suitable answers.
   i) Rusting **ii)** Burning

2. **a)–c) In any order.**
   a) Measure the amount of reactants used.
   b) Measure the amount of products used.
   c) Observe or measure the formation of a precipitate / colour change.

3. **a)** X. The line is steeper than Y and therefore the reaction is faster.
   b) i)–iii) Accept any three of the following: Surface area of solid reactants in X is greater than in Reaction Y; temperature of reaction X is greater than Reaction Y; a catalyst is used in Reaction X but not in Reaction Y; concentration of solution in X is greater than in Y.
   c) That one of the reactants is used up and the reaction has stopped.
   d) The same amount of product is formed from the same amount of reactants.

Pages 77–78

1. **a)–d) In any order.**
   a) Temperature
   b) Particle size or surface area.
   c) Concentration
   d) Use of a catalyst.

2. **a)** They move quite slowly and do not collide that often, so fewer collisions are successful.
   b) When a mixture is heated, the particles move more quickly and collide with each other more often and with greater energy, so more collisions are successful.

3. **a)** Particles are spread out – they collide with each other less often resulting in fewer successful collisions.
   b) Particles are crowded close together – particles collide with each other more often, resulting in many more successful collisions.

4.

	Surface area	Collisions	Reaction rate
Large particles	Small	Few	Slow
Small particles	Large	Many	Fast

5. A catalyst is a substance which increases the rate of a chemical reaction without being changed itself during the process.

6. **a)** Slowly **b)** Fizzing

7 **a)** They move a lot faster.
   b) There are many more energetic collisions and they happen more frequently. This means that the minimum energy required for reaction will occur more often, leading to a greater rate of reaction.
   c) More frequent collisions and more collisions that are sufficiently energetic for a reaction to happen.

8. Lowers the amount of energy needed for a successful collision.

9. It is not used up during the reaction so can be used again and again.

10. **a)–c) Accept any other suitable answers.**
   a) Carry out a complete risk assessment of the chemical synthesis and take the necessary precautions, e.g. buying necessary safety equipment.
   b) Must have a high enough rate of manufacture to produce a sufficient daily yield.
   c) Does the chemical synthesis produce any harmful by-products that impact on the environment?

Pages 79–80

1. Energy; matter; energy; travels; longitudinal / transverse; transverse / longitudinal.

2. **a)** For a transverse wave the pattern of disturbance is at right angles to the direction of wave movement, while for a longitudinal wave the pattern of disturbance is in the same direction as the direction of wave movement.
   b) i) Sound waves **ii) Accept either** light **or** water waves

3. The frequency of a wave is the number of waves produced (or passing a particular point) in one second.

4.

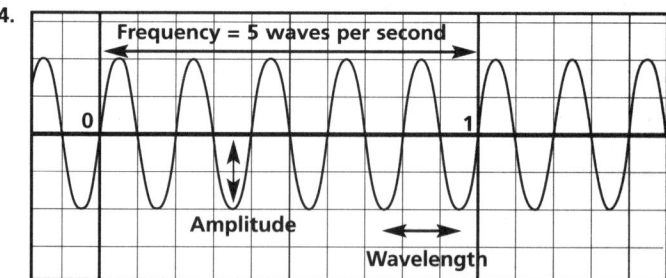

5. If the frequency is increased, the wavelength will decrease. If the frequency is decreased, the wavelength will increase.

6. If a wave slows down the wavelength will decrease.

7. Wave speed = Frequency x Wavelength

8. **a)** iv **b)** i **c)** iv

9. **a)** 300 000 000m/s **b)** 0.25m **c)** 6×10^{16}Hz

10. 3m–3.1m

Page 81

1. **a)–c) In any order**
   a) Reflection **b)** Refraction **c)** Diffraction

2. When a water wave crosses a boundary between one medium and another there is a change in wave speed, which causes the wave to change direction.

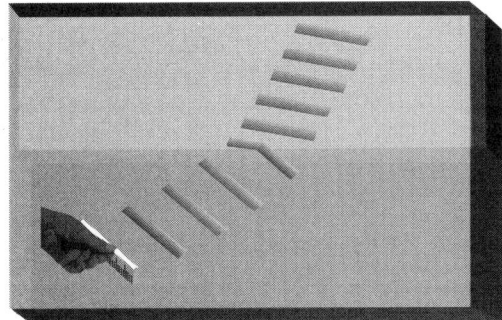

3. a) This means that they spread out from the edges.
  b) Nothing, as the wave would not be diffracted. The wave would continue at the same speed and in the same direction.

4. The sound waves from the transmitter would be diffracted round the hill and so would reach the house. Light waves can only be diffracted when there is a small gap so in this instance the light waves would not be able to diffract round the hill.

5.

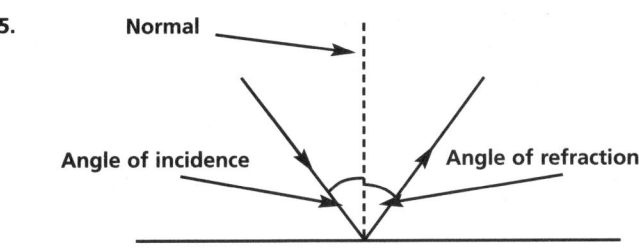

6. i) The incident ray is the light ray travelling towards the mirror.
  ii) The reflected ray is the light ray travelling away from the mirror.

Page 82

1.

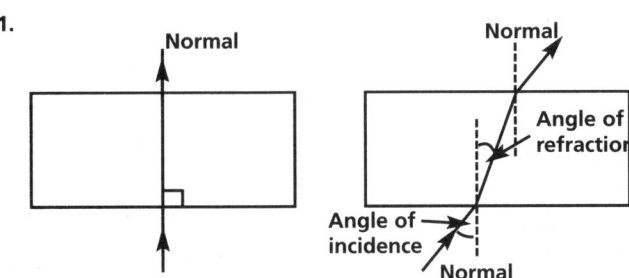

2. When a light wave passes from one medium to another the wave speeds up and is either refracted towards or away from the normal so it changes direction.

3. Total internal reflection. The light ray is unable to leave the medium and is reflected back.

4. a) True **b)** False **c)** False **d)** True

5. Several smaller waves could be in step and their crest height would combine to create a freak wave with a very large height, and a deep trough. This would be very dangerous for ships and would be able to sink even large ships and ocean liners.

Pages 83–84

1. A photon is a packet of energy.

2. e, b, d, f, g, a, c

3. a)–c) In any order.
  a) Sounds waves are longitudinal, whilst electromagnetic waves are transverse.
  b) Electromagnetic waves are much faster than sound waves.
  c) Electromagnetic waves can travel through empty space, but sound waves need a medium to travel through.

4. 300 000 000m/s

5. The amount of energy carried by each photon.

6. a)–b) In any order.
  a) They can be reflected.
  b) They can be refracted.

7. a)

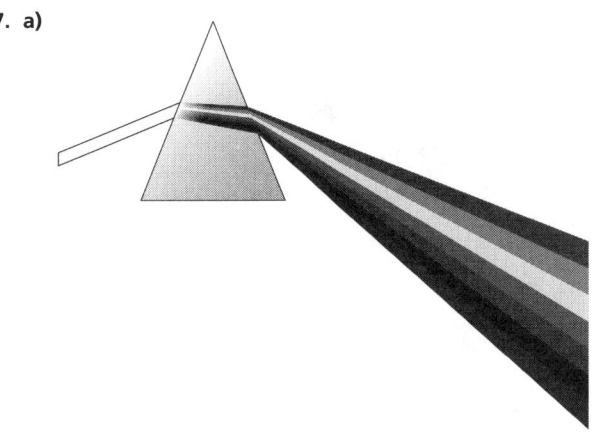

  b) White light is made up from many different colours which are diffracted by different amounts by the prism.

8. Radio Waves – Transmitting radio and TV programmes.
Light and infrared – Carrying information on computer networks and telephone cables.
Microwaves – Satellite communication. Heating food.
X-rays – Taking shadow pictures of bones.

9. Microwaves are well reflected by metals so satellite dishes are made of metal and shaped to reflect the signal onto the receiver.

10. X-rays are absorbed by dense materials so they are therefore suitable for 'seeing' inside bodies and objects. They are used to produce shadow pictures of bones and to check luggage at airports.

Pages 85–86

1. a) Amplitude modulation. The input signal causes the amplitude of the carrier wave to change.

  b)

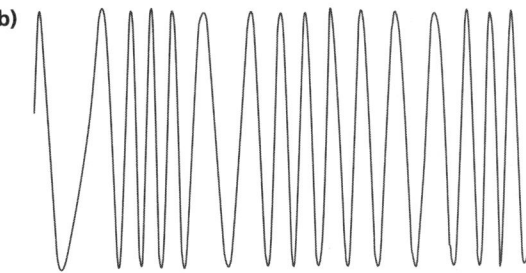

2. An analogue signal can have many different values, whereas digital signals have two states, on (1) or off (0).

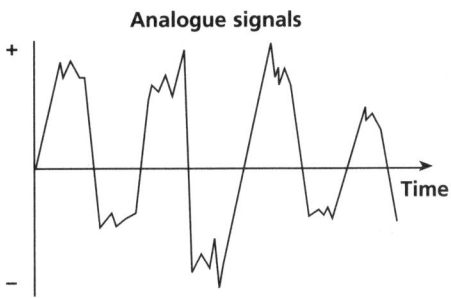

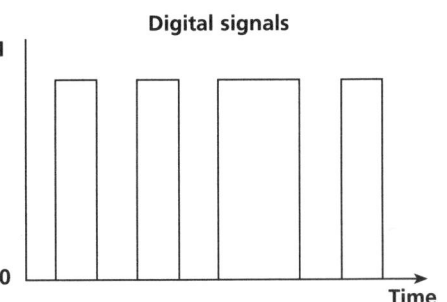

3. Accept any height for the value of 1.

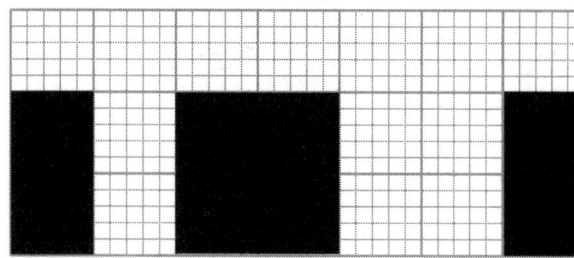

4.

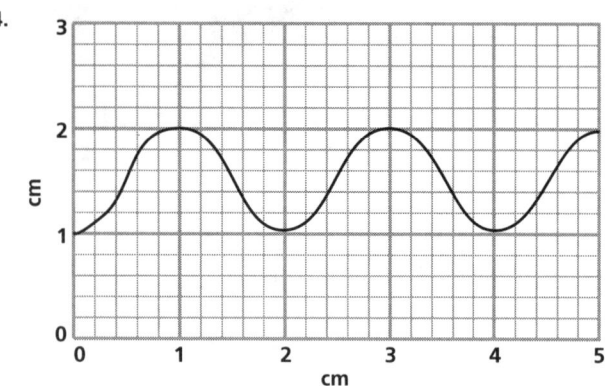

5. Signal noise is the random variations that signals pick up when they travel. This reduces the quality of the sound.

6. Digital signals have two states, on and off, which can still be recognised despite any noise that is picked up. Therefore, it is easy to remove the noise and clean up the signal, restoring the on / off pattern.
Analogue signals have many different values so it is hard to distinguish between noise and the original signal. This means that the noise can't be completely removed and when the signal is amplified, any noise picked up is also amplified. This can lead to a hissy sound.

Page 88

1. a) iii

b) The scans showed that autistic children have enlarged head sizes by up to 10%
c) Larger head size.
d) i)–ii) In any order.
  i) Social skills **ii)** Communication skills.
e) The neuron pathways grow too rapidly to process sensory and motor experiences so the pathways are not strengthened and retained. Therefore, no experience is gained.
f) A child is lacking stimulation or has not been exposed to the necessary experiences.
g) Learning a language later in development is a much harder and slower process.

Page 90

1. a) X-rays scanners 'see' inside bags to look at objects.
b) ii
c) No. It would be easier to detect as they have to be kept in a container which has a defined shape.

2. Electromagnetic analysis could be used to detect explosives which are hidden inside electronic equipment. A swab could be taken and analysed to see if the vapours of the sample contain traces of the chemicals commonly found in explosives, such as nitrogen.

3. a) i)–ii) In any order.
  i) Nitrogen **ii)** Hydrogen
b) They both have a low atomic number.

4. A photon is a packet of energy.

5. Low frequency.

Pages 91–92

1. a) Acid
b) i) Alkali **ii)** Series **iii)** Reflex
c) i) Digital **ii)** Mitosis **iii)** Osmosis
d) i) Effector **ii)** Velocity
e) i) Amplitude **ii)** Resultant
f) i) Hypothermia **ii)** Specialised **iii)** Alternating
g) Fertilisation

2. See Wordsearch below for highlighted answers.

P	A	A	L	T	E	R	N	A	T	I	N	G	A	L	J
A	B	O	C	R	X	Q	B	D	V	E	S	I	U	E	P
K	W	P	H	H	S	U	A	N	E	L	I	E	D	N	I
A	I	G	M	F	W	R	C	K	L	L	S	U	O	T	H
M	Q	A	L	K	A	L	I	Q	O	S	O	Q	B	P	F
P	D	R	I	Y	R	M	D	V	C	N	T	C	E	E	M
L	A	O	S	F	D	B	O	D	I	A	I	J	R	R	T
I	I	S	S	E	P	I	U	H	T	Z	M	T	E	S	O
T	M	M	V	D	R	X	B	F	Y	B	I	S	D	T	X
U	R	O	R	T	Y	I	K	D	F	L	U	A	I	R	M
D	E	S	E	H	I	M	E	I	I	L	S	O	G	G	D
E	H	I	F	E	B	G	L	S	T	Z	R	B	I	F	V
E	T	S	L	N	L	D	A	A	D	P	Y	N	T	J	J
G	O	P	E	B	F	T	N	T	Q	K	Q	J	A	X	I
A	P	T	X	S	I	T	S	H	G	R	T	M	L	B	S
I	Y	A	L	O	T	Q	G	S	J	L	Y	B	H	R	P
N	H	E	N	K	P	F	W	V	B	R	H	M	P	D	G
P	D	T	O	Q	R	O	T	C	E	F	F	E	G	U	X
K	O	D	E	S	I	L	A	I	C	E	P	S	C	M	Z
V	B	B	Q	V	N	Y	F	N	P	S	A	I	U	J	K

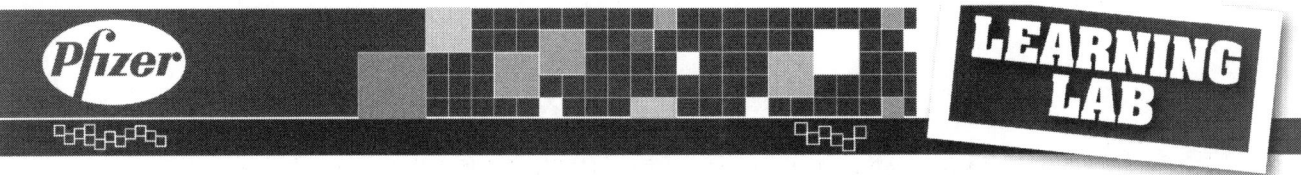

She Expected the Best Day of her Life.
It turned into a nightmare!

Just imagine

You are representing your country at an international sporting event. It is your proudest moment but then disaster strikes. Four of your team mates die, many are injured and you are left fighting for your life.

Deadly fungus

The collapse of a makeshift bridge at an event in Israel sent 16-year old tennis player Sasha Elterman and 60 of her Australian team mates plunging into a heavily polluted river. Sasha was

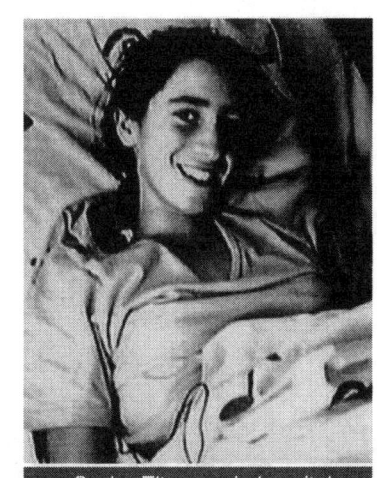

Sasha Elterman in hospital
"I'm very grateful to Pfizer"

pulled from the wreckage but not before swallowing toxic sludge. A rare, deadly fungus known as *Pseudoallescheria boydii* attacked her brain and spine. She was given only a three percent chance of survival.

Who could help?

Over the next few months Sasha was kept alive by existing antifungal medicines but she didn't get much better. Then her medical team heard of a powerful new drug from Pfizer that was still being trialled. Sasha was given the medicine for 451 days.

Did the medicine work?

At the 2000 Olympics in Sydney, the young athlete, who was once given almost no chance to live, carried the Olympic Torch to the cheers of her fellow Australians.

Who saved Sasha?

Hundreds of scientists, statisticians, technologists and medical professionals helped Sasha find her road to recovery and win the game of life. Many of them work for Pfizer, discovering new chemical compounds to tackle disease, then turning them into medicines. Every day two million people in the UK take a Pfizer medicine.

The Workbook

The Essentials of GCSE OCR Additional A Science

This answer book should be used to mark pupils' responses to the questions in *The Essentials of GCSE OCR Additional Science A Student Workbook*.

Westmorland House, Elmsfield Park, Holme, Carnforth, Lancashire LA6 1RJ
Telephone - Sales: 015395 65920 General Enquiries: 015395 65921 Accounts: 015395 65922
Fax: 015395 64167 email: orders@lonsdalesrg.co.uk web: www.lonsdalesrg.co.uk

ISBN 1-905129-95-5

9 781905 129959

Published by Lonsdale A Division of Huveaux Plc